In Mortal Memory

ANDREW MCNEILLIE is a Professor of English at Exeter University's campus in Cornwall, having previously been Literature Editor at Oxford University Press. He recently founded a new literary magazine *Archipelago* which provides the focal point for an MA course, 'Writing, Nature and Place'. His memoir *Once* was published in 2009 by Seren. His books include *Nevermore* (Oxford *Poets*/Carcanet, 2000), *Now, Then* (Carcanet, 2002), *Slower* (Carcanet, 2006), the prose memoir *An Aran Keening* (Lilliput Press, 2001) and a biographical memoir of his father, *Ian Niall: Part of his Life* (Clutag Press, 2007).

Also by Andrew McNeillie from Carcanet Press

Nevermore
Now, Then
Slower

ANDREW McNEILLIE

In Mortal Memory

CARCANET

First published in Great Britain in 2010 by
Carcanet Press Limited
Alliance House
Cross Street
Manchester M2 7AQ

A CIP catalogue record for this book is available from the British Library
ISBN 978 1 84777 084 4

The publisher acknowledges financial assistance from Arts Council England

Typeset by XL Publishing Services, Tiverton
Printed and bound in England by SRP Ltd, Exeter

for Diana Maureen Porter

i.m. les neiges d'antan

Acknowledgements

Some of these poems have appeared in: *Agenda, Alhambra Poetry Calendar, Archipelago, Arète, Oxford Magazine, Oxford Poetry, PN Review, The Reader, Scottish Review of Books, Southlight, Times Literary Supplement* (including the complete sequence 'O Vos Omnes'), *Yellow Nib*. The editor of *Archipelago* aside, I am grateful to the editors of these publications for their encouragement. The poem 'Boozy Weather' appears in the photographer Jemimah Kuhfeld's 'The Poet Project'.

Contents

PART I

Song in Winter

I saw the Spring return, when I was dead...
William Wordsworth

Winter Song

(i) *Chanson d'hiver*

I lie awake for more than half the night,
like a northern summer, my mind suffused
with light, though it's deep winter still
and long days are a dream that's yet to come
when short nights keep a bonfire never quite
gone out. I call this hope, if you will.

An oystercatcher on a roof-ridge pipes
night ashore and day aboard in light
like wreaths of smoke; and, even from this far,
I can hear the tide crunch packed air,
quarrying the bay for white sand.
What is it that I cannot say, to you?

It's not that I dislike the cold air:
rain turned to sleet and flakes no longer hesitant
blinding the headland with light,
like a poke in the eye with a sprung twig,
and metaphor stranded for the duration
out in the wilderness of frozen pipes.

The world as it is I can take if it exists,
as appearances, and commonsense, insist.
But they always insist too much, the facts
and certainties their own undoing,
for life is all becoming, and this winter night
I lie here wide awake because of you.

(ii) *Road Closed*

This morning in January jumps
at the woodside, and the world rocks
as if hungry for the vernal equinox.
Headlong we go. Nothing damps
our appetite for change. Time ticks
too slow. Who can abide it
hanging so? What once was valid
is no longer. Who doesn't know?

Sheared branches fly, and ivied limbs
break under the weight of air,
blocking the road. Pensive or vacant, we queue,
out of sight, and into mind. The view
explodes and tugs, as at heart strings.
And beyond our fish-tank staring-out
it hurls ahead, reckless of destiny.
As, just to think of you, my heart hurls me.

(iii) *Winter*

Winter has nothing to offer but itself.
It is the year's last resort, though holly
come into berry and mistletoe offer relief
to deciduous life and the ancient sky.
Winter will do for me, the thing itself.

(iv) *The Shadow of a Blackbird*

It wasn't snowing and it wasn't going to snow.
Snow had become a thing I used to know,
a metaphor whited out of every latitude I knew.
So when it crossed my mind, I thought of you.

So winter might have looked to its laurels,
no longer variegated, no longer what it was.
And the blackbird stranded in its branches
looked the shadow of a blackbird too.

(v) *O Wood!*

This wood-and-leafmeal air,
dank and frosted, deadens
and scours the earth, as if
for signs of life. They're
somewhere, I tell myself,
wired to the weather.

Disturb my heart? I am already
wrecked beyond belief,
whichever direction you turn me.
O wood! would I were ever
as certain of rebirth
from such wreckage, as you are.

Those who would put
a Stoic face on it, I number
well, their wood for trees.
I'm of their timber,
but I know their belief
isn't all that it appears.

(vi) *February Song*

It was a false evening
very like a dawn.
I heard a songthrush singing
from an empty thorn.

Something in the light
encouraged it to sing
and as it sang so I have sung
and been as wrong.

(vii) *Les Feuilles d'automne*

Autumn leaves, packs its bags,
and winter inherits empty trees.
Metaphor as symbol begs
to embark again on violent seas.

What put the no in November
won't be gainsaid.
No more I, though I remember
mal de mer and wishing to be dead.

No more I, whatever that might mean,
before the sea's ego.
Everything and its season
gone before you know.

(viii) *Uneven Song*

Winter trims the gas under the Michaelmas daisies
and purple turns to ash.

Once ripe with promise, October fails
and sinks into November's darkness.

I knew you in my guilty innocence
when autumn was no corruption.

Then even winter fell to earth to rise again
in frosted brilliance.

The prototype of spring and resurrection
promised like seed-time in its first green season.

But, in inverse proportion now, eavesdropping
on an Oxford evensong

and prayers of repentance,
I step into the dark content to be brought to nothing.

(ix) *Tidings*

In the long nights I began
as if setting out for spring.

Making preparations for the bride.
Laying all bare.

I lingered bitterly through Easter,
then gave up the ghost, on the weather's cross.

What might have been cannot be written off,
as being without meaning.

I'd lived for something more
but will make do with loss.

(x) *Spinney*

These are long days now,
though winter days are short,
prey to frost, and even snow,
or uneven, migrant north,
rare as winter lightning
used to be, chasing death.

Like a blood clot in the thinning light,
thickening up, vestige after-glow,
with angioplastic blackbird
scolding through, memory
false and true, to free the heart
from where it cannot go.

Boozy Weather

What I think I'm doing here, killing time,
in this London hotel bar, I do not know,
the evening bustling in early May,
the streets thronged with passers-by.
Too early, surely, to talk of winter?
But brooding as I sip Grey Goose vodka
I glimpse a skein of wild geese as they cross
a wintry sky... On which high octane
lost trajectory, I find myself, and leave
the world behind, back in my comfort zone
of cloudy weather, where possession is
all tenths of the law, and I am dispossessed
of here and now, and all my little grief,
for half an hour or so, seems what it is,
mere *comme il faut, encore une fois...*
and not why is the world the way it is?
But these others, in their happy hour,
laugh, as if they'd laugh for ever,
passing their drinks through the air, to one another...
in the press at the bar. Boozy weather
it is for them and the heart in chaos
weighs anchor for the evening's crossing
to a happier oblivion than any seems
possible to me, for my sins, in which
I don't believe, and sorrows, which I do.

Grief

If forgetting were an option
what would you choose to purge?
Did anyone ever put such a question,
the offer you can only refuse?

Here, now, where evening thickens
into night, I cling to light
at its diurnal death. Brackens
feather the headland. I forget

how often… But I forget nothing
about you, and remember as if
you were everything
though now that everything is grief.

How Deep is the Ocean?

It is my sixty-first year to my doom:
I am at sea and more or less alone.
There is a place I commonly call home.
There are some folk I love to call my own.
I know some fragments of a heartfelt song
that tells how every day man lives and dies.
There is a broken net I trawl along,
a leaking haul of fishy memories.

I have a code I tap when things go wrong
as fog rolls in or waves climb out of sight.
I know the mirage and the siren song
but still the dream farewell, at setting out,
allures, and back-ashore's look-bright.
As if I know what death is all about.

High and Dry

This vessel is unreal, forget
the starry archipelago.
Those haulers... how
they bore her up through
the dune, I don't know.

So I bear this, and turn it,
roof-up, to keep a secret,
safe from winter, aware
some of us won't see spring
together, whoever we are.

Time's here by the sand grain,
in abundant galaxies,
an excess of it, like memory
paint-stripped, on a salt wind,
bringing tears to the eyes.

Les Poètes maudits

Between salon and saloon: a porthole,
in a *paquebot*, a late moon passing over,
making its crossing between
l'art pour l'art et mal de mer
and no one to talk to but oneself
reading the cursed poets in parallel text.

The nib of the ship pauses in mid-air,
then plunges on, into the inky morning.
All reality's a journey. All coasts
are fictions and all harbours symbols.
Cursed and blessed we go
to see what we believe, good hypocrites.

i.m. Juliette Drouet

Of all of them I would have preferred you:
like those backing girls in Motown
I adored in youth, or Mary Magdalene
(forgive me, please…) and still do:
heroic girls with walk-on do-wop roles,
victorious victims of the powers that be:
dream-women who make it through
to *papier maché* dignity, as flesh fails.

I want to spend the night with you,
soirée à deux, you in all your finery,
shabby-genteel, glitter of old jewellery,
remembrance found in your lost gaze,
and you will tell it like it was
to strut your stuff, and play the muse.

Love in the Language Room

A room three storeys up
and many a story round
where ungainly albatrosses we
tried to leave the ground
as if speaking in tongues
dans le nord du pays de Galles.

Sexe et tristesse
à côté de la mer,
là-bas-longing to be elsewhere,
aground on Dogger Bank.
Not everything's translation
or there'd be no originals.

In the spirit is the letter.
So I come to you,
my heart laid bare and
dictionary in hand
with my story in my native tongue
for you not quite to understand.

Le Rêve

i.m. Villiers de l'Isle D'Adam et Pauvre Lelian

Must be lived in to be lived out –
stepping from Le Gare du Nord –
whatever its gender, however
housed, or homeless, under no roof
but the sky, above your misspelt heart.
How many of them came this way?

Arrival is also departure.
I am fluent in that grammar,
I should say, before you start
to put me right. Fluent, I say,
le mot juste, where otherwise
no justice saw the light of day.

Solo in New York

The pianist-singer plays and sings
'I'm beginning to see the light'
though night has fallen, dark brings
reflection to glass and to the heart,
aided by Scotch on the rocks.

Always that beginning charms me
and not 'I can't get started…' now,
as the rhythm section kicks
inside my head and I begin to blow
my solo here, my ballad elegy.

A brief riff above Park Avenue,
'Solitude' my bride, thinking
as I write of no one else but you
as one who's seen the light
and cannot help but sing.

Summer Reading

Upheaval of the heart, turmoil
like revolution brought to grief.
Then Second Empire censorship,
a new regime, an exiled life…

Haunted and shadowed
exquisitely all summer.
What has Nostromo to do with it
but a lighter of silver to launder?

My Death

In the year of my death, given notice,
the days will be bigger, and the nights.

In the season of my death
the weather also, and the griefs.

In the month of my death I'll haunt
three places, unless I can't.

In the week of my death
I will say my farewells.

On the day of my death
I'll not know what day it is.

In the hour of my death
I will breathe my last breath.

Mislaid

I found it in the new grass
a song thrush egg and pricked it
with a haw thorn
and blew it out as I'd not done
in nearer fifty fitful years'
remembering.

Then the orange yolk still
tacky on my fingers,
I fumbled for my notebook
and my pen
to prick at it again
where life had been.

Trick Cyclist

The journey we're all on
to oblivion, and sorrow,
for others and ourselves...
I muttered to myself,
driving along in the rain
when round the corner
I overtook a man cycling,
head cocked against the rain.

Something about him,
a strangeness, his oilskin
very like my own,
made me check the mirror
to study him more. But
when I did he'd gone.

The power of desire is so
displacing and there's no
accounting where the mind
might go in its disturbances,
the reason all unspoken.
I'd seen myself there. But
where I was going and why
are no mystery.

At 'The Oystercatcher', Portmahomack

Under whose name I dine this evening,
a world away from the world, in July,
in far-flung Cromarty, where blink and
you'll miss night as if stung in the eye
by a snowflake, one lost winter's day.

The skies across the firth tower smokily.
North dreams beyond in pillows of fresh linen.
It's late but not too late to dream of you
curled up in night, head on pillow,
dreaming whatever you dream now.

I'm dining with a local fisher who tells me,
of all people, what I know already:
that the oystercatcher doesn't simply pipe
but sings too… Of what? Immortality,
time and tide, and sorrow.

Literalist

The thrush deceives no one.
The curlew betrays no one.
The lark inspires no one.
Ravens never say never.
Nor does the yellowhammer
sing about bread or cheese
in the beggared hedgerow.

The stormcock's no herald.
The terrace peacock isn't proud.
The nightingale never ravishes.
Swallows in number
don't make a summer
nor the wild goose skein
bring autumn again.

Spring Campaign

Spring has no business here this month,
or so you'd think, this damp cold morning,
as the brisk couples, ramblers with maps
hung round their necks, ornithologists,
pensioners with dogs, all come and go,
about their constitutionals at Blenheim as
a gunshot resounds the length of the Estate
and cold as a brass monkey the Duke
stands upright on his column.

On Woodstock Lake, two men fishing in a boat
keep warm by burning charcoal in a can.
Its smoke hangs on the air and drifts
as they drift, in a haze or trance,
as later glimpsed through trees, all gauze
before my eyes, and in the water. Briefly,
I imagine black-powder cloud and carnage,
courtesy of which I dream along
thinking of you, and of the spring.

Like titmice flitting in the crowns of trees
I go, with even less than Lilliput
to my credit, my purposes obscure
beyond mere exercise and habit,
pausing to scribble in a notebook
the premonition of this poem for you
withheld, as at this time, everything
in the day denies by glance and light
something, reveille, I think I'll call it,
that one dawn soon will fill the air.

The Rising of the Year

The one you'll never hear again.
The one you'll never see.

But were you to get lucky
you wouldn't be mistaken.

There'd be no embarrassment
and no disappointment.

No short shrift as might be human
after so long but as if only

yesterday they left off calling
like the faithful ones they were

night and morning
at the rising of the year.

Hedger

A true hedger hedges no bets,
bending and cutting, warp and weft,
thorn and ash, sycamore and hazel,
his barricade to all but light,
pour encourager les autres…
come spring's uprising of the heart.

Great Leveller

To migrate into versatility before
Mont Sainte Victoire not Parnassus.
To be alert to altitude sickness
and to prefer *mal de mer.*

The mountainous sea the great leveller
but above all, beneath all,
to keep the watch, the vigil,
and your course, to tack, and weather.

Internal Exile

Visitations, hauntings, travel…
a journey North
overnighting in the Isle,
lodged at the Steampacket
on the harbour wall.
Better to arrive than travel
though arrival's mythical
and comes with baggage.

Botanical Gardens Revisited

I saw the Spring return, when I was dead...
Wordsworth

A fine spring day. The morning shines.
Too much billing and cooing to doubt
the future of pigeons, or humanity,
in this sanctuary from an uneasy world,
even for my unquiet heart. Sap thrives.
Take those two settled by the fountain with a picnic...
as if to rub my nose in it, they stand,
link arms and, glass-to-lip, drink
to each other with their eyes, then
mouth-to-mouth what's his is hers.
... Russian-style, I think, or Polish. But
seeing they sense my staring sorrow,
I flinch, and look back at my book.

Nightjars

I wavered like the hour itself, eyes giving way to ears
as owls and woodcock in a blur
flitted through shadows of thin air
but never a nightjar joined them.
I stayed there waiting, none the less,
still learning things about myself,
the same things as usual. When
from nowhere the air filled with nightjars
rising with a whipcrack, and churring
as if possessed
jamming the airwaves, until I felt
lost there on the heath
among the Nissen footings and flooded pits
and ghosts of airmen.

Arctic Terns

Just so, there are towns where
arctic terns nest in the square
and last light harbours keep
night and sleep at bay, as
I remember, and remember you.

How incongruous congruities
make for beauty, uniquely.
Ever to see you again might
elude me, other than in memory,
among the fishing towns of the heart.

Anno Domini 2007

I watched a pair of thrushes build their nest
in a laurel in my garden.
Stealing out now and then
as they had stolen in
I checked their progress,
first in building, next
when five eggs in the hen bird
started brooding
and at evening rain or shine
her partner sang.
Stealthily I stepped across the lawn
like a thief to see and not be seen.
Strong recognition I felt
but what was I recognising?
Remembrance, tenderness,
in this dark year of our lord?

Summer Migrant

Here, again? And no doubt,
and no doubting the difference
between us. For habit in you
is truth. What you repeat
is beauty, to the senses.
But mine is deadly,
seeking solace, needy, and
dependent on such fleeting
appearances to forget.

The Big Snow

Just when you've cracked it
and worked life out
and how your little luck makes sense
enough, you take a hit.

Think of it as shipping a wave
out of the blue,
never due or overdue.
Think of it as falling in love.

The Wild Thorn

The day stands on formality,
timing its entry, like a bride.

How could she be late?
What might that be beside?

What suspense of cloud.
What gauze, and hand to hair...

PART II
At Sea

It is generally well known that out of the crews of whaling vessels… few ever return in the ships on board which they departed.

from *Cruise in a Whale Boat*, quoted in *Moby-Dick* by Herman Melville

Life-Line

Be sure that you've secured it at both ends.

The Voyage

poem on Mandelshtam's birthday

Trust to the day and to your craft.
Send the old quayside caveat
'Weather Permitting' to hell…
Turn three times anti-clockwise
in your swivel chair, or on your heel,
only the daïmon or the muse
controls the tides. 'Poetry's a mystery,'
so wrote the poet's widow
from the heart, knowing the worst,
having looked it in its steely eye.
This isn't one of Stalin's barges,
up to the eyeballs, stark-staring mad.
No matter the world is
staring at apocalypse.
Embark! Set sail…!
What though we may never meet again?

Night-Snow

wee song for Sydney Graham

The real poem never ends.
The blizzard beneath its last footprint
is where we search in its memory,
the blizzard that is also night
as fresh on your face as snow.

Night-snow the ultimate
a body must weather, body I say,
but I mean soul
out on the manhole sea
where the littoral-minded sail

beyond Cape Metaphor to be.
And Sydney Coastguard keeps his watch
ticking on course for Greenock,
with Alfred Wallis at the wheel
aboard the good wreck *Alba*.

For who but a blind one can't see
Scotland from Cornwall? –
every small hour of the year
with the heart in the right direction
and a glass to his eye.

from *A Night on Whalsay*

1

It is one thing for the mail not to come
another for nothing to come in the mail.
I'm not talking about love but words,
reading matter, news from the wars,
the latest collection by a great poet.
Don't talk to me about inner resources.
I too have had the Atlantic at my door all night
and my hearth the only thing between me
and the bareforked cold. Even the stones need light
to fall on them, and wind and tide to rattle them,
so they're never for a moment the same.
Just so, it's mistaken to say nothing has stirred
except for rhetorical effect, to catch
the idea of a flitting shoreline bird.

2

On the stillest morning and human kind
nowhere to be seen, but as you see yourself
front down, or your shadow walking before you
travelling westward to the rim of the world
and not a breath to flap your coat-tails
on the heart's shingle shelf. Not a breath
but your own, a life for once of your choosing,
whatever its hardships and downsides
as you step out, the world stripped to
essentials of sea, sky, shoreline, and bird –
infinity's limits. So island life intensifies
and shoots its net in the belly of the whale
and day and night you make your haul
come in and grow like so many bright herring.

3

Many a night, not just this one, I spent with you,
long since you died. I hear your father
poses for van Gogh these days, his true last look
yet to be seen. He'd have needed nine lives anyway
to deliver the sorting office of your mind,
and we're still waiting, parting the net curtain
for sight of the *paquebot* coming at last
leaping like a salmon, a mile high off West Linga
or far-flung Tory Island in a storm by Dixon.
Not archipelagos but arpeggios the *mot juste*:
spirit and letter one and the same,
in true haecceity. Live in the mind
the life that lives the dream
and leave the ground, for the ground of being.

4

Without which where'd we be? Too much at home.
It is one thing to call and find a person out,
another to visit without calling. They say
the dull-at-heart, you never spent a night in any sea cave.
Truer to say you hardly put your head down anywhere else,
unless on a hillside to interrogate the thistle.
As if art and truth could be literal-minded
except by design and history's what happened.
It's not all in utterance or we'd be too overcome
to speak, but it is only in utterance
that things can be known and only in art remain
irreducible, open as the gates of a bird,
or the bottle I set down on midnight's kitchen table
to speak this, in mortal memory.

5

Of wilderness and keeping watch. Prophets
without honour in their country.
Taller seas than those beyond your window.
Ever more perfect storms. The thing itself,
in all life's brevity held at bay, where at last
the mailboat hoves in view, floating and soaring,
to deliver word of the world, manna heaven-sent
at your wind-battered door.
Its departure a rehearsal to delay thought
as once again it makes its exit, here through
a curtain of blown rain white as snow.
So one day for the last time it will ferry you.
But you barely look up, scribbling in your bunk
at the mind's stony limits of value and meaning.

6

Elsewhere, appeased, extremes clash.
Perpendicular armies strut their grief,
beyond a southern sea. True North is here,
where the heart's stayed, with mosses, comforted
with lichen, north of the wall; and winter sunlight
thrives, as thrives the human spirit in its wood,
at Hallaig, or by the deciduous Atlantic
off tree-bare Inis Mór, at Catraeth, as you said:
the invisible war, also a war of words.
Whose are we? Whose were we? Under what names
must history steal its march at our expense?
March meaning also a wall, a border or boundary,
as with Spring in our step we take new hope,
perennially, indomitable, human cost.

7

Now the present is heritage and history and
holiday in its season knocks at the door
of Grieve House, to look at your absence, grieve not.
There's no going back and who'd want to?
Even poetry has no reverse gear, though it
circumnavigate the ground of its being forever.
Even science works only in hindsight
slower than the speed of light preoccupied
with nature and origin, in dead time.
So what are we here for in this hovel winter,
this hopeful spring, this *hafod* summer,
this mist of autumn but to hold forward,
with courage and to sing according to our gifts,
as if we could do otherwise by act of will.

8

In my book that's not a question, though
to some it might be. I cannot speak for you.
It's a rule of grammar for one thing and
democracy for another, but in ventriloquy like this
who can tell where the voices come from,
articulating what for whom? No island is an island
entire of itself. Depopulate, regenerate...
the tidal rhythm insinuates everywhere:
the ground bass, with those twirly bits of yours,
bead-proof grace notes in the great music.
Don't ask for whom the bell tolls: it's too obvious.
The small hours we call them, as if to steady our nerves,
but they're the biggest of all.
No wonder nature prefers we sleep the night away.

9

Nature would make short work of us all
but the muse is always one step ahead.
She keeps the bottle pouring and the ink
regardless of the hour and ordered life.
The nights I've spent subject to her charms
are few enough but still I've had my out-of-body moments
scribbling to the rhythm of her intellect
and passion, mooching round harbours
with her on my arm as if we were lovers
destined for each other. She tells me song is being
and life both genial and tragic; that poetry
begins with an inner fact of consciousness;
and urges me to outsail the storm,
make landfall leagues ahead of elegy.

10

How self-imposed poverty spells freedom.
How poetry and poverty are almost the same word!
And both constrain to set truth free.
How you knew that… the inner fact of being
that holds its value forever, like gold.
I treasure the memory of my time still
and it's not too late to invest in it again.
Late though it is and not a matter of style
but of being and necessity, not to sleep on one's watch,
but keep the vigil singing along in the dark,
beyond the comfort zone, against the build-up to
farewell. For it's six in the morning again
and already the first ferry of the day
has let go fore and aft to catch the tide.

Netting the Scottish Fish

Not so many miles north of Cawdor
nor in the worst of tide or weather
the netsmen aboard their coble
and their fellows on the cairn,
study every fold and quibble
of light on water through July...

Never naming what they look to see,
they call a fish a fish, from superstition.
And today again the unnameable
remains ineffable, invisible
to all but the inward eye. A condition
with a long history here.

The Lilies of the Field

This country is my barricade,
my doorway and my heart's hearth.
Yet accretion and erosion attend
everywhere, as we live and breathe:
the world is all coming and going.

But for half the night last night
I had the Plough jammed in my skylight,
and the earth stopped turning,
as if god said: hold your horses,
consider the lilies of the field.

Casting

Have no eye for anything but keething.

Keep your mind as empty as your creel.

The only clockwork the windings of a reel.

The only minute the one you're making.

Clockwise or anticlockwise gaze

through no more than 180 degrees.

No eyes in the back of your head but

a moment's hindsight and reflection

can surprise deepest circumspection.

Trout are not the only things with eyes.

Hackles up and *qui vive* for the rise.

Here's a hook to hang life's beauty on.

Synge-Song

I was one after your own heart
or so I thought, neither landed
nor gentry, but blew ashore
aboard your limpid pages,
to Inis Mór and there I stranded.
My mind blown away
and all at sea for nevermore.

The curragh also wears a thin partition.
I've felt the sea-pulse beneath it
through my hand, life itself,
inside out, outermost to be
inmost in the world.
Get out more, you who say
poetry makes nothing happen.

Be-in-the-world and see:
the poem is earthbound
and elsewhere to the day
as any playboy knows
down the passage of recorded time
through calm and storm
the first to make landfall.

O Vos Omnes

to G.H.

(i) *Baudelaire: 'Quelques caricaturistes français'*

Walking in the other place, the poet
turned and said to me, 'Daumier
kept me going.' My search engine
ran on apace and brought me *inter alia*
not, as I'd guessed, to an august salon
but stuff about redressing wrong, the cretin
man in all his folly. (Nearby grave men,
without gravamen, haunted the architecture.)

And I ran on, a dog at heel
(pauvre chien désorienté, sans but
et sans pensée), detaining him as best
I could with foolish chatter. Uphill
all the way? At times I wonder
what the point of life is. Tell me, poet?

(ii) *Homage to K.D.*

Why do I think of Germany here? Witness
and conscience fell from the same tree,
the grafted *Apfel*. He strode on before me
like a great bear foraging through stars.
I told him what K.D. said of Günter Grass:
'He lied to win the Nobel Prize...
It was the lie itself, and not its cause:
we could all and many have lived with that.'
His brother ripped apart *Deutschland über alles*
in the star-spangled style of Jimi Hendrix.
But for cello. How German is that?
'They should not have bombed Belgrade.'
To find ourselves in such a state...
we've seen the best of our times, I'm afraid.

(iii) *i.m. Donato di Niccolo Donatello*

The upright shall live through faithfulness.
                                        Habakkuk

'I don't need anyone,' he said, severely.
Thank you, I thought, and raised my glass
to my lips, pausing for reflection. Why
for god's sake am I doing this?
I looked my Acheronian oyster in the eye
and slurped it down. Bits of gritty shell
yet might make in time a pearl.
You'd have needed an oysterman's knife
to open the silence now upon us. Life
in death, or death in life? You lie,
I thought, you lie, remembering the roll-
call from Donne to Gurney,
Rosenberg to Rose. You need the dead.
'... The Habakkuk blew me away,' as he said.

(iv) *i.m. Sion Hill*

Nothing between us and the Urals? Nothing?
Cast your mind back. What memories are these?
Nowhere this side of Siberia bleaker skies
than I remember fieldfare and redwing
starveling darkened in winter's cold war.
Box-like de Havilland and Meteor
screeched across, ready for the worst.
Soldiers wolf-whistled my mother from a lorry.
Men touched their caps. Manners oppressed.
Hard to know what we think we mean by peace.
Never say worst, there is none? No less sage,
never say best? There was no golden age.
Yet in-between, no small part of the story,
how break of day can still seem blessed...

(v) *End of the Line...*

I'd be wary of pastiche, if I were you,
I said to myself, wondering. But he phoned
that night and urged me on, praising a new
technical advance, regarding enjambement.
Heavy losses sustained to peace of mind.
The lift-shaft of self-doubt yawned.
Work as I might I could not go beyond
the end of any line, for even a moment.

For days I stared as if at years between
advances, the same as spoke volumes
of laboured silence in those times.
Don't go there, *comme on dit*, but play the clown?
I too am a very different poet from
the one I used to be, whatever iamb.

(vi) *Alms and the Man*

Gurney and gunnery, too close for sanity.
Deep in darkness, he was himself once
on a gurney, electro-shock therapy
the morning's menu... Stunned into sense
not new to his experience. He was himself
once, or so he says – granted glimpses
of providential beauty, like Hopkins, his synapses
wired so. Google came up with nothing
like it in twice the time. He was himself
and after no one sang his song.
He never sought asylum from the world
but had it thrust upon him. Greatness
raved and after no one sang his song.
Alms and the man our sorrowful refrain.

(vii) *Bedside Reading*

In Waterstone's stocking up on novels –
I mean detective fiction – poets don't
read novels, or write them, because they can't.
Name one? They're always something else.
Making ready for the long day's journey
into night, and no poem in the offing,
the game up, the Daïmon withholding.

I thought he might cease at any hour.
No tide-table. No return fare. No special
rates for parties travelling together.
No reservations, except those you'd call natural.
It's a short ride but while you can see
the wake of the ferryman, you've as long
as it takes to come and go there.

(viii) *Spleen et idéal*

The flotillas thronged, heavy as ever.
It was like Venice in high summer
but juddery in Dunkirk-black-and-white.
No leeway for casuistry… We sat
talking towards evensong. 'I hate,'
he said, 'the post '45 generation…
They betrayed literature, despising what they taught.'
Original sin the subject of his sermon.

Sins of emission thickened on the air.
We rode it out and railed against the shits,
leavening our fear with spleen.
'I wish I was dead,' he said. And Charon,
after Henry, made reply: 'My friend, you are…
As far as immortality permits.'

Commemoration

And how far is it, the other journey? –
to resurrection day, the reception committee
in attendance at the pierhead,
reciting to the air in sure and certain immortality
verses on a newly unveiled plaque.

Here lies one whose name is writ in stone
who set sail decades back in cloudy weather.
Now at the heart's funeral, some words
under a cloud, grief for a reckoning,
a balancing of books, the verdict not guilty.

Cnut 2008

Leaning back, as if pulling at an oar,
his throne a-tilt, and his crown awry.

Never mention land-words at sea,
he recalls, an old superstition.

So his latest: never mention
sea-words ashore.

Aswim

The sea furled and unfurled
on the flags, wave and rock.

Only look at it and it floods back
the makings of this world.

The wall-maze another leviathan
and light falling as rain.

Cloud-wash. More stories than
you could shake a stick at

if you could find one
unless washed up ashore

sea-smooth, rubbed down
like Brendan in mid-winter.

In the Midst of Life

for Gail

in homage to Patrick Conneely

Or mist, I dreamt myself alive again, back from
the dead, beachcombing down that wintry shore,
lit by a sea-candle's orange-iodine flame –

the bay drawling, like a conch at my ear,
sea spray and salt wind whirling, and the dunes
whistling in a gooseflesh shiver of marram.

The day was like a night with no moon,
and the air crustacean, clawed; had there been a bell
it would have tolled, ask not for whom.

It isn't fanciful to think, heaven and hell
got married that morning, bride and groom,
and I there uninvited, one long-ago drowned

beyond space and time, in Blind Sound.
So seawards, singing my sea-words to the world,
flotsam-jetsam, heart's kindling, I strode –

with voices in my head, or not, I couldn't tell.
But both, the answer was, not either or.
'What a memory you have,' he said, and smiled.

He didn't know the half of it. Though he'd hand-hauled
in twenty fathoms the better part of his days
and seen such changes in a body's fortunes

would shake faith down to the rock of ages.
'Fish stocks recover, left to their own devices…
It's never too late. But what can you do with the weather?'

The fog flurried our *mise-en-scène*. (Enter: a polar bear,
adrift on an ice cube.) 'Curtains for us all!'
he cried, 'and they say we still have far to fall…'

Then he said, 'You know, I think those were *better* days'
and glanced as he spoke, weighing his words,
to the last syllable of what it is to know poverty.

Involuntarily, my mind flashed, like a night at sea,
aglitter with stars and villages ashore, barely lit,
and shipping lights, freighted with memory.

I struggled to agree but knew grace required it
and to be true to my heart, I said I feared it was so.
How can you live with so little fishing to look at

leaning on the sea-wall of old age? I don't know.
Winter indeed, the only tourist-free zone,
winter and its slender hold on light.

But you don't need to be old to be deranged, just
thin-partitioned from looking askance at life
and its short way with us all from the start. Mad

in the style of Father Ted, who now has his day,
his little immortality, when fancy-dress priests
and nuns invade the island, to party wildly.

It being our duty to laugh in the face of grief.
Yet to know which comes first and what it means
to name so many lost at sea and still believe in life.

And who knows what else might come to pass
to catch our leisure by the heels and wake us
from our sleep?... The sea was in and now the plane

roared on the runway at Cill Eine, then took to the air
like a swan in reverse. As if to prove that
you can turn the clock back. And now 'Somewhere

beyond the sea...' the crooner croons
to Saturday night, singing so long ago...
Prize what's new, I say, but give me retro too.

'I know beyond a doubt...' he purrs... but
nothing will be as before, however many moons
go quartering the tides to make a haul of silver.

True places aren't down on any map, said Ishmael.
Thoughts run, beyond the page, and do not fit.
White is the colour of truth? So of the whale

that's never found on Ahab's map but in his head?
Never say never, nor either or? But both, I think,
inner and outer; and seize the hour's the trick.

For myself I was born in Thermidor. Unlike Patrick
Lobsterman, I'd sooner tire of life than lobster-meat.
But the sea is always greener, not to say the drink.

So with his sea-green hair Charles Baudelaire led
thought on a leash through the streets of Paris,
and sang so long ago, 'Somewhere beyond the sea…'

Là-bas… his bittersweet melody divine.
No matter the barman stands forever calling time.
Drink deep but keep your head above water.

As out here the islands keep theirs and prosper
while earth's luck lasts. Only the immortal poor,
and their poem, have footing that is surer.

However far into the hour you row dreaming
you'll wake from your senses. But waking may I
never hear you sing: 'Never again will I go sailing.'

Though now the curraghs are made of fibre glass,
and they have outboards… What is it in
habitude's reciprocity? 'No more canvas!'

Patrick laments. The quick pulse within,
inboard swell of ocean felt athwart,
dancing cheek to cheek, and sea to skin.

For intimacy's the best we have by heart.
Had I a hand for it I'd paint his portrait,
in oily impasto of sea-surge and cloud…

But this instead. Like poetry, fishing's an art, I said,
and when we put out to shoot a net
or spill a line, we do it with both thought

and craft, one stretched to the other, taut
but not too taut, as to be merely formal,
with give and take, between wave and boat.

As here and now, the soul's recital
turns on an oar, and comes full circle.
On holiday in Sardinia he bought sea bream.

So once he caught them here, in autumn,
but never now, their stock fished out,
though time may yet shoal them back again.

He felt at home, islanded, and hearing 'Irish' in
the slap and splash of the Med, and loved at dawn
to see fresh fish landed, as for the first time.

Just what the thing itself must be about
when the scales fall from your eyes and you see
your life flash by. Then out goes the light…

What might be *better* days? Don't get me started.
True and untrue to say they lie ahead
as in the first line of a poem poised to be written.

But to say at once farewell, fare forward, and
haste back won't do. For all is nothing new.
I folded the money and put it in his hand

and thanked him for his company. He shook his rein
and the pony 'Grace' struck out for home, hoofbeat
for heartbeat… remembered all the way again

that tattoo round the bay, and down the strand,
where beachcombing for metaphor I meet
that one with a torch still burning in his hand.

i.m.lah

There is no darker hour and you've fled North,
I like to think, haunting where I'd love to stay.
But my train speeds south, in the wake of storm.
So in the wake of you, my heart careers
to think how in the midst of death, I am in life,
witness to your obsequies, come Wednesday.
No one can stay and leave. But as you know
it works the other way. The image in the jimmy-mirror,
with just a wipe of the hanky stays
eye-bright for eternity… Just so your poems run,
like the river at my window, and can't be late, or early,
however fast or slow they make their journey.
But always and forever now, they go, and stay,
strong in themselves, as you were at leave-taking…

And would you put that one in your drawer?
Then pluck it out for print, months later,
to surprise me when a column fallen short,
at the hour's last ditch, needs filling at its foot
with an inch or two – pitched against purity,
sprung from the fount of our shared grief?
… Choose life? O *Flying Scotsman*!
The lesson of poem-spotting jumps all points
and *caesurae* like the purest drug or drink
ever distilled to the page. What else? Please ask
when next you see them: Dunbar and Burns,
Hogg, Scott… MacLean and Hay, MacDiarmid…
what other route you might have taken
out of this earthly station and still been here in time?

Seaworthy

What would change the way we think?
Not much, and too much to ask.

No good to say, step back from the brink,
but plough into the dark.

Even the best craft takes a lifetime
to turn round, into seaworthiness.

And on the way, many a drowned rhyme,
and many an SOS.